HELLO, BABY!
I'm Your Mom

BY EVE BUNTING ⸱ Illustrated by JUI ISHIDA

PUBLISHED by SLEEPING BEAR PRESS™

"Baby darling, you're so sweet!
Your tiny hands, your tiny feet!
I love you. I'll take care of you
like other loving mommies do."

"Hello, my little kitty-cat.
I'm your mom. Imagine that!
I'll share my nice soft bed with you.
It's cozy and there's room for two!"

"Soon, I know, you'll fly away.
Till then we'll cherish every day.
I'll bring you bugs to make you strong
and sing you songs the whole day long."

"I'll show you how to snap your jaws
and use your tiny little claws.
I'll stay with you and watch you grow
and teach you what you need to know."

"Your skin is wrinkled, just a bit.
Another month and it will fit.
Not everyone will look at you
and think you're pretty, but I do."

"My pouch is ready, just for you,
my little baby kangaroo.
It's soft and warm and close to me.
How lucky can a baby be?"

"I've checked your paws and checked your teeth.
You're striped on top and underneath.
I'll teach you how to hunt alone
when you are grown and on your own."

"Baby mine, swim close to me,
through this stormy, restless sea.
Don't worry about tides or weather.
The sea is ours. We'll swim together."

"My darling little porcupine,
your quills are soft, but they'll be fine.
They'll soon be sharp, and that's okay.
We'll hug each other anyway."

"Hello, my little elephant,
I'm your mom and that's your aunt.
That's your sister, grandma, too.
They'll help me to take care of you."

"My precious, tiny polar bear,
it's cold outside, but we don't care.
Our den is warm, and when you grow,
we'll hunt together in the snow."

"Ever since the world began
this has been the perfect plan.
Hurrah for moms and babies, too!
I was a baby. So were you!"

Hey, did you know?

Cats spend 70 percent of their lives sleeping, which is around 13-16 hours a day. That's a LOT of catnaps!

If you're a rhino, you don't have to be old to have wrinkles. Even babies have wrinkly skin. In some parts of their body, the skin can be approximately one and a half inches thick.

Birds love bugs and eat a lot of them. You'll find bugs like these on the bird menu: beetles, flies, ants, grasshoppers, and crickets. YUMMY!

Young alligators generally stay near their mothers for the first year of their lives, but it is not uncommon for some to stay close for up to three years.

Because their babies are born very small (about the size of a lima bean), kangaroos have a special pouch that serves as a "nursery." The baby stays in the pouch for about six months.

Stripes do more than just look good on a tiger. They help camouflage the big cat so it blends in with trees and tall grasses.

Mixed in with their soft fur, porcupines have long, sharp quills that protect them from predators. When they are born, their quills are very soft, but they harden within a few days.

Although whales live their lives in water, don't call them fish! They are mammals, just like humans. They breathe air and are warm-blooded.

Polar bear cubs are usually born between November and January. The bears' body heat helps keep the den nice and warm. In late March or April, mama bear and babies emerge from the den.

In elephant families, an older, experienced female is in charge. A family usually contains a mother, her sisters, daughters, and babies (calves). There are always plenty of babysitters!

For Christine . . . wonderful mother to Anna,
wonderful daughter to Eve

—Eve

For all moms and babies, cubs, pups, kittens,
calves, chicks, joeys, piglets, hatchlings . . .

—Jui

SLEEPING BEAR PRESS™

Text Copyright © 2022 Eve Bunting
Illustration Copyright © 2022 Jui Ishida
Design Copyright © 2022 Sleeping Bear Press
All rights reserved.
No part of this book may be reproduced in any manner without the
express written consent of the publisher, except in the case of brief excerpts
in critical reviews and articles. All inquiries should be addressed to:
Sleeping Bear Press
2395 South Huron Parkway, Suite 200
Ann Arbor, MI 48104
www.sleepingbearpress.com
© Sleeping Bear Press
Shutterstock photo credits: kangaroo: Anan Kaewkhammul;
kitten: Petr Jilek; porcupine and polar bear cub: Eric Isselee;
rhinoceros: Neelsky; bird: Joseph Scott Photography;
whale: Imagine Earth Photography; elephants: Efimova Anna;
alligator: Kristina Vackova.
tiger: Jeremy Bishop on Unsplash

Printed and bound in the United States
10 9 8 7 6 5 4 3 2 1

Library of Congress Cataloging-in-Publication Data
Names: Bunting, Eve, 1928- author. | Ishida, Jui, illustrator. | Title: Hello, baby! I'm your mom | by Eve Bunting ; illustrated by Jui Ishida.
Description: Ann Arbor, MI : Sleeping Bear Press, [2022] | Audience: Ages 0-4. | Summary: From a wrinkly baby rhino to a kitten's cute paws,
mothers love their babies just as they are. Back matter includes photos and factoids about each featured animal.
Identifiers: LCCN 2021037586 | ISBN 9781534111462 (hardcover) Subjects: CYAC: Stories in rhyme. | Parent and child–Fiction. |
Animals–Infancy–Fiction. | Love–Fiction. Classification: LCC PZ8.3.B92 He 2022 | DDC [E]–dc23 LC record available at https://lccn.loc.gov/2021037586